Sounds good

Other titles published for the Council for the Care of Churches by Church House Publishing:

Church Extensions and Adaptations, 2nd edition

Church Lighting by Peter Jay and Bill Crawforth

The Churchyards Handbook, 6th edition

The Conservation and Repair of Bells and Bellframes: Code of Practice

A Guide to Church Inspection and Repair, 2nd edition

Historic Organ Conservation

A Stitch in Time: Guidelines for the Care of Textiles

Stonework: Maintenance and Surface Repair by Alban Caroe and Martin Caroe, 2nd edition

Towards the Conservation and Restoration of Historic Organs

Sounds good

A guide to church organs, for incumbents, churchwardens and PCCs

John Norman and Jim Berrow

CHURCH HOUSE PUBLISHING

Church House Publishing
Church House
Great Smith Street
London SW1P 3NZ

ISBN 0 7151 7594 7

Published 2002 for the Council
for the Care of Churches of the
Archbishops' Council by Church
House Publishing

Copyright © The Archbishops'
Council 2002

Type size: 9.5/11 Sabon
Printed by Halstan & Co. Ltd
Amersham, Bucks

Contents

Illustrations

Preface

Inside most churches the pipe organ is undoubtedly the largest and most expensive single item of furniture. A good pipe organ, well maintained, is a sound investment.

Although cathedrals and larger parish churches have often had pipe organs for many centuries, in most churches organs began to appear only from the middle of the nineteenth century onwards. There are today many examples of fine instruments built in the second half of that century which still give good service and will continue to do so throughout the present century. An impressive number of new organs are also built each year, often replacing earlier instruments whose integrity has been lost in the past through unsympathetic or inappropriate alteration.

Like any piece of machinery and engineering that contains moving parts, organs need regular servicing throughout their lifetime and, at longer intervals, cleaning and restoration. However, many of those charged with the responsibility of maintaining the fabric of a church, whilst being sensitive to the needs of organs, will have little knowledge of the issues involved or of the technical language and terms that they will encounter when reading reports from organ builders or advisers.

John Norman and Jim Berrow's excellent and useful booklet is designed to help just such people: those who find themselves involved in making decisions about the future of a pipe organ but who need help and guidance not just in understanding the technical aspects but also in assessing the range of options which are likely to exist for the most appropriate way forward. The booklet gives clear information and advice on all aspects, as well as containing an invaluable glossary giving simple explanations of technical terms.

Those who read this booklet and follow through the recommendations and suggestions given by John Norman and Jim Berrow on how best to proceed will be well prepared to reach wise and informed decisions for the organ in their own churches.

Alan Thurlow

Chapter 1
Introduction

Why an organ?

The organ goes back a thousand years in the service of the Church, and back to antiquity in its invention. The practical reason why it became an important part of divine worship is that the organ produces a greater variety of sound than any other single instrument. The alternative of several performers on different instruments needs a multiplicity of players who require to be organized and rehearsed. The wide range of the organ between very soft and very loud can suggest emotions from quiet contemplation to a great outburst of joy. Its flexibility makes it relevant to many different styles of music. The sustained sound provides more support to the human voice than any percussive instrument: it has proved the best way of leading the singing of a large number of voices. This has remained the basis of its use in Christian worship, especially in the last 150 years.

The primary purpose of organ music in church is to accompany worship. The requirements are, in order of importance:

1. Leading congregational singing;

2. Accompanying the choir (if there is one);

3. Solo performance to enhance the mood of worship at appropriate moments, and the performance of suitable entrance and exit music.

What is an organ?

The organ is a wind instrument but is unique in having a separate pipe for each note. The pitch of the organ can reach both the upper and lower limits of human hearing. Different sorts of pipes provide variety of tone. These are controlled by 'stops'. Each stop normally brings into play a complete and independent set of pipes.

PIPE SHADE

FRONT PIPES

MOUTH

SWELLBOX

SOUNDBOARD

STOP-KNOBS

MANUALS

RESERVOIR/BELLOWS

PEDAL-BOARD

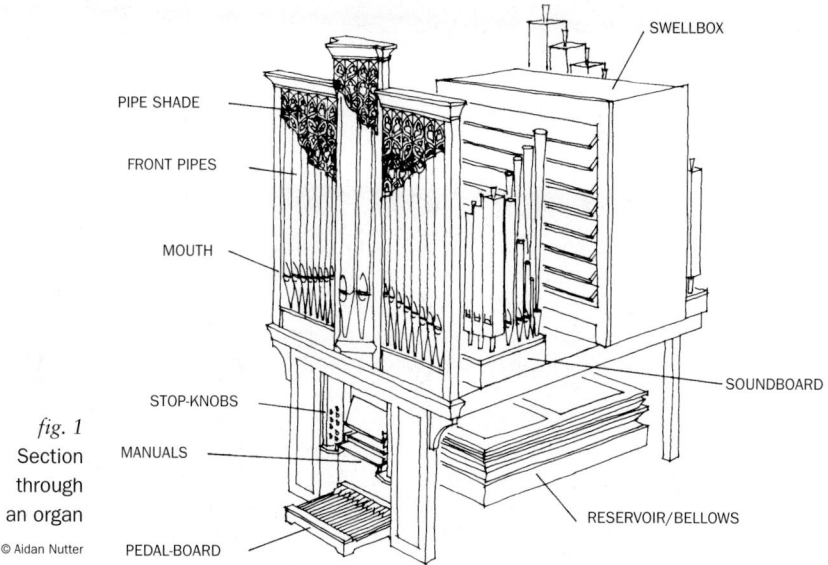

fig. 1
Section
through
an organ

© Aidan Nutter

With all the different stops, a parish church organ may well
contain over 1,000 pipes. The development of the organ has led
to individual designs for each building, matching the sound to
the acoustics of the church and the number of pipes to the space
available. For flexibility in playing, the pipes are often grouped
in separate departments, each with its own keyboard, so that
players can quickly switch from one sound to another. The
largest and deepest-toned pipes are usually played with the feet
from a pedal keyboard.

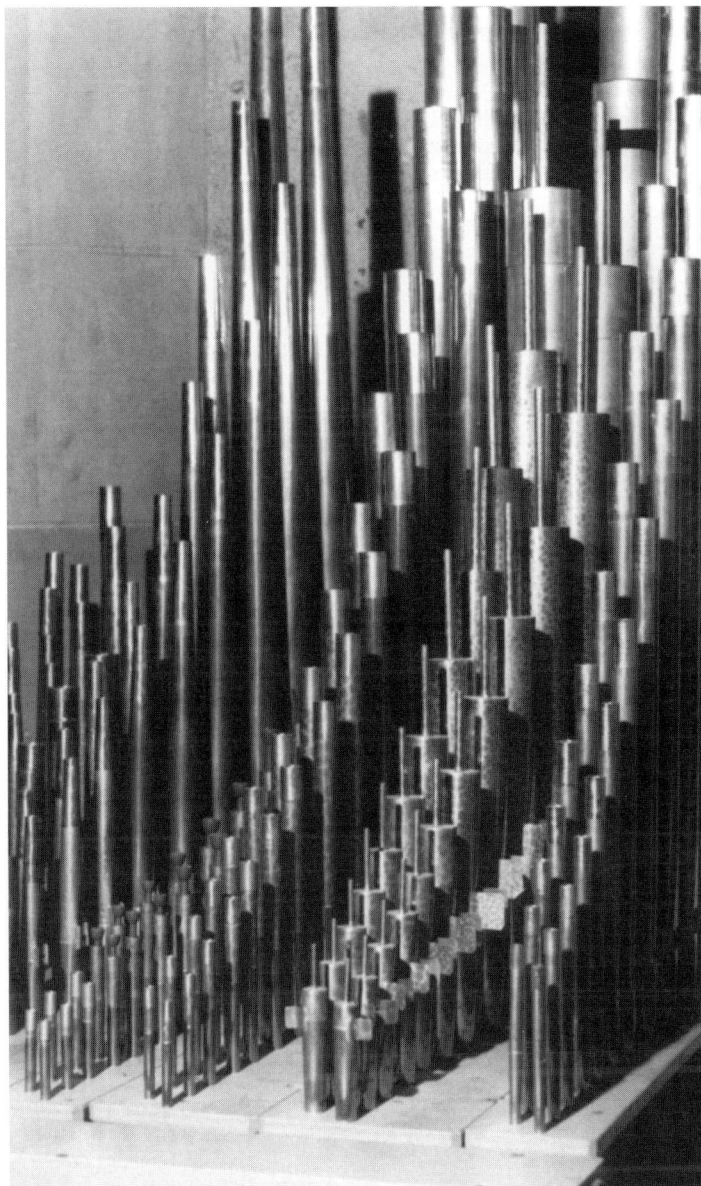

fig. 2
Pipes on a
soundboard

Alternatives

Other instruments available to perform a similar role are the harmonium and the American organ, which use vibrating reeds instead of pipes, and instruments that use electronic simulation of organ sound instead of pipes. More details of electronic instruments are given in Chapter 7 (from p. 22).

Care

An organ is usually the largest and most expensive piece of furniture in a church. Nevertheless, properly cared for, a well-made instrument will give service for many years. Century-old organs, in good working order, are still relatively common. Organs work best when kept away from extremes of heat and humidity.

Roof leaks can cause expensive damage, as can access by unqualified persons. Organs should be protected if decorators are working above them and when building works generate significant amounts of dust. Do not introduce large areas of carpet into the church; they can upset the acoustics both for the organ and for singing. More information on caring for your instrument is given in Chapter 2 (p. 7).

Maintenance

Parish church organs need relatively little maintenance and regular use is beneficial. Tuning and adjustment are needed more often if the instrument has been allowed to get into poor condition. Eventually, after thirty years or more, the dust that accumulates inside the instrument will need cleaning out. More information on maintenance is given in Chapter 2 (p. 8).

Repair

Over very long periods, moving parts will wear and leather parts will lose their strength. Straightforward repair is nearly always possible. Organs may also need repair if damaged by rain-water leaks or, in the case of older instruments, by low winter humidity. Further information is given in Chapter 3 (from p. 10).

fig. 3
Bellows

© Aug. Laukhuff

Historic instruments

A church may possess an instrument of historic value. Old organs, like old buildings, often contain parts from different dates. For example, a historic case may contain a relatively modern organ. In any event, special care is needed to avoid inappropriate alteration and consequent destruction of value. A guide to identification is given in Chapter 4 (p. 13). Information about grants for the repair of historic instruments is given in Chapter 11 (p. 31).

New organs

There will be occasions when it is appropriate to consider the provision of a new organ. You will find a checklist of things to do if you are undecided between repair and replacement on page 12. Advice is often available from denominational advisers or independent professionals (see Chapter 9, p. 29). Sometimes a second-hand organ may be suitable, though many are too bulky for modern churches. More information on second-hand organs is given in Chapter 6 (p. 21).

Where space is a particular difficulty an electronic instrument may be the only answer. These are extensively advertised and have low initial costs. This advantage has to be set against a relatively short replacement cycle and wide variations in quality between makers. Further details are in Chapter 7 (from p. 22). One of the merits of a new organ with pipes is that, since all organs except the smallest are individually designed, the layout and appearance can be designed to complement a particular church. Any organ should be a visual ornament to a church as well as a musical one. More information on new organs is given in Chapter 5 (from p. 16).

Organ-builders

It is important to employ an organ-builder whose talents and accreditation match your requirements. Hints on selecting organ-builders are give in Chapter 8 (pp. 27–8).

There is a glossary of technical terms in Appendix 1 on page 32. Suggestions for further reading and useful addresses and websites are listed in Appendices 2 and 3 (pp. 37–8).

chapter 2
Care and maintenance

Environment

Organs are made of natural materials such as wood and leather, and work best when kept away from extremes of heat or humidity.

Avoid:

- Direct heat or sunlight;

- Heating the church all week to over 16°C; organs made before about 1930 were not designed to withstand the drying effects of modern winter heating and old soundboards will be damaged by timber shrinkage. If continuous heating is unavoidable, the installation of an organ humidifier will help protect the soundboards. Modern organs are less sensitive.

- Too rapid changes of temperature; high-speed heaters can cause problems. The temperature in an organ in an elevated position can reach 25°C when the temperature on the church floor is less than 15°C. This not only wastes fuel but can cause tuning and mechanical problems.

- Roof leaks; although general damp causes little harm, dripping water can cause expensive damage. If the damage is not repaired, some stops may not work and the air supply may become variable, so that the organ will tend to go out of tune. The cost of repair may be recoverable under the church insurance policy.

- Using the inside of the organ as a cupboard. Damage may be caused to the instrument and maintenance access impaired.

The sound of an organ is heavily influenced by the acoustics of the church. Any changes to the acoustics will affect the sound of the instrument, as well as that of sung worship. The introduction of large areas of carpet will make a major difference to the acoustics and independent professional advice should always be taken before installation.

Maintenance

Parish church organs need relatively little maintenance. A small organ without reed stops should stay in tune for at least a year.

Reed stops need more frequent tuning because they react to temperature changes in a different way from the remainder of the instrument and may need tuning twice or more each year.

Organs also need more frequent attention if the soundboards have been allowed to get into bad order, causing variations in the wind supply to individual pipes.

Organ tuners should make minor adjustments to the action as part of their work. It is good practice for the organ to have a tuner's log book, in which the organist can record any faults in tuning or mechanism and which the tuner can sign after his visit. Minor faults, such as notes 'off' or sticking 'on' or noisy wind leaks, should be taken up with the tuner in the first instance.

Organs gradually accumulate dust inside them. This eventually builds up to the point where the speech and tuning stability of the pipes is impaired. Cleaning is needed about every thirty years or so, though it can be required earlier if the organ is not properly protected when church painting or other building works are in progress. Organ pipes are mostly made of a tin–lead alloy that is very resistant to corrosion but sensitive to physical damage. Only qualified persons should be allowed inside an organ.

Reliability

If you are experiencing problems:

- Talk first to your organ tuner – it may be a problem that can be fixed inexpensively.

- If major work is recommended, consult the organ adviser appointed by your denomination.

- Prepare brief for organ-builders.

● Research the reputation and relevant accreditation of possible organ-builders.

● Seek quotations from up to three organ-builders.

● In choosing, remember that you are making a decision for a generation or more; quality of work is therefore paramount. Cut-price work is often more expensive in the long run.

● Submit the specification of work from your preferred organ-builder to your Diocesan Advisory Committee or other relevant body.

● If approved, seek Faculty or equivalent.

● Place order.

Hints on dealing with organ-builders are given on pages 27–8 in Chapter 8. Information about Faculties is given on page 29 in Chapter 9.

chapter 3
Repair

Organs last an amazingly long time. There is no reason why an organ which was well made in the first place and is undamaged by external conditions or foolish alteration should not last indefinitely. Nevertheless moving parts will wear and leather parts will eventually lose their strength:

- Bellows leather commonly requires replacement after 100 to 125 years as does the leather surface of other internal parts, unless previously damaged by water penetration.

- The small leather bellows used in pneumatic action require recovering after 40 to 70 years, depending on the design and on the quality of leather.

- The felts and working joints of a mechanical 'tracker' key action usually require replacement after about 70 years.

- The pedal keys of a well-used instrument may require repairs in 30 years.

Repairs are often combined with the cleaning of an organ; money is saved if the two jobs are done at the same time.

Pneumatic actions

The repair of organs with tubular-pneumatic actions can be a problem. Some organ-builders have little experience of them, and if the lead tubes that are the heart of these actions have been poorly run and have sagged it may cost less to replace the action than to repair it. Nevertheless many well-made pneumatic actions can be repaired by organ-builders with appropriate expertise.

Electro-pneumatic actions

Electrical parts often need attention after about 50 years and the low-voltage wiring may require replacement. There have been many improvements in the design of electric action in recent years and it is not unusual to replace the coupling action and the combination action rather than to repair it.

Mains-voltage wiring

Do not allow electricians to run mains-voltage wiring fixed to the organ case. In particular, avoid adding unsightly switches or light fittings to the cabinetwork of the organ console. Try to locate them sensitively elsewhere. Treat the console like any other piece of good furniture.

Additional pipes

There is often pressure from musicians for additional ranks of pipes to be installed at the same time as an organ is repaired.

This is usually a mistake, except where planned as part of the original design of the organ and omitted for economy. Additional pipes nearly always complicate the mechanism and make servicing access more difficult and expensive. If pipes are voiced in a different style from the original, the result is usually musically unsatisfactory, as the blend between the different voices will be upset.

Detached consoles

Technical developments in the twentieth century made it possible to detach the console and move it some distance from the organ. However, the cost of cabinetwork and additional mechanism will be substantial. If the congregation is nearer the pipes than the player, the balance of sound as heard by the player may be very different to that heard by the congregation. A console more than 40 feet (12 m) from the body of the organ will suffer from acoustic time lag, introducing considerable difficulties for the player. Any console more than about 10 feet (3 m) from the organ will involve the use of electric or electro-pneumatic action which is both less responsive and less reliable than a mechanical key action.

Moving an organ

Liturgical re-ordering may suggest that an organ be moved within the church. This is no minor matter as complete dismantling will be required. Such a move can affect both the sound of an organ and its appearance, and these consequences will need to be thought through with all relevant parties. Further advice on organ position is given on page 16 in Chapter 5.

Checklist when deciding between repair and replacement

- Consult your denominational adviser.

- If advice is positive as to the course of action, prepare brief for organ-builders and then proceed according to the checklist on page 9.

- If advice is conditional, prepare outline briefs for each alternative strategy.

- Do research on the reputation and relevant accreditation of possible organ-builders – these may not be the same for each strategy.

- Seek quotations from up to three organ-builders.

- In choosing, remember that you are making a decision for a generation or more. Electronic instruments may help to solve space problems but are usually more expensive in the long run.

- Submit the specification of your preferred course of action, with detailed drawings, to your Diocesan Advisory Committee or other relevant body.

- If approved, seek Faculty or equivalent.

- Place order.

Hints on dealing with organ-builders are given on pages 27–8 in Chapter 8. Information about Faculties and other denominational control systems is given on page 29.

chapter 4
Historic organs

Churches fortunate enough to possess a historic organ are the trustees of an irreplaceable part of our national heritage. The Newman Report to the Government recommended that special attention should be paid to such instruments and that each denomination should compile a list of them.

Which organs are historic?

A historic organ may:

● form part of a complete furnishing scheme in the church;

● contain significant quantities of pre-1800 material in a later instrument;

● have been made before 1860, even if modified later;

● be the work of a noted builder between 1860 and 1900, even if the mechanism has been altered;

● be an organ of definite quality, without significant alteration, made between 1900 and 1940.

Organs built over 30 years ago can also be considered historic if they show technical innovation or virtuosity, or have associations with well-known characters or events.

It is good practice to know the history of your organ. The National Pipe Organ Register at Cambridge University now lists most organs and is available for consultation over the Internet (www.bios.org.uk/npor.html).

fig. 4
St Mary at
Hill, London
(William Hill,
1848)

Maintaining historic value

Old organs, like old buildings, often contain material from different dates. Particular features or individual components may have historic value, even though the organ as whole is not historically important. Nevertheless, historic instruments need special care to avoid inappropriate alteration. Once integrity is lost it can never be fully regained. Do retain original parts if possible or, where replacement is essential to the continued functioning of the instrument, use similar materials to the original.

Avoid:

● replacing or re-voicing original pipes;

● replacing original action mechanism with new mechanism of a different type;

● replacing ivory key surfaces with plastic substitutes or introducing modern typefaces to stop controls;

● introducing tuning slides, where not previously fitted, without independent advice;

● trying to fit modern pedal-boards or balanced swell-pedals to consoles not designed for them;

● trying to fit modern playing aids, such as combination pistons, to historic organs not designed for them. In addition to destroying historic value, such changes are usually expensive.

Do:

● employ an organ-builder with an IBO Historic Restoration accreditation OR who has a known reputation in the restoration field.

Inappropriate alterations can prejudice the eligibility of historic instruments for grants from public bodies. A full record of all restoration work is an essential part of work on historic instruments and is usually a pre-condition of grants.

chapter 5
New organs

New organs may be needed:

- for new churches;

- where the previous organ has suffered a disaster;

- where the existing organ has been so poorly altered or maintained that it is not worth repairing;

- where the organ now needs to be placed in a very different position within the building;

- to replace a life-expired electronic instrument.

Organ position

It is important to consider the position of a new organ very carefully. If there is a choir, then organ, organist and choir should all be together and within reasonable distance of the congregation. If possible, the organ should be a free-standing piece of furniture. Free-standing organs speak out better, take less room (because they need less in the way of internal passageways) and are easier to move or sell if circumstances change. Although bass sound will go round corners, the higher pitches that determine tone quality travel largely in straight lines. It is better to have a small organ in a good position than a larger one forced into an out-of-the-way location. Divided organs, either side of the church, are possible but expensive.

Size of organ

The more stops an organ has, the greater the range of tone colours available, so some players press for as large an instrument as possible. Nevertheless, a church with a 'live' acoustic will need only a relatively small organ if this is placed in an open position; such an instrument will sound far better

fig. 5
Box organ
(Kenneth Tickell)

than a larger instrument tucked away in a chamber. An organ that is too large for the building will either be too loud or will need to have each stop muted somewhat, losing character and life in the process.

Appearance

The organ should be a visual ornament to a church as well as a musical one:

● A good organ case can justify a prominent position for an instrument.

- An organ case should be rather like a large wardrobe, enclosing the instrument on all sides, with the front filled with decorative pipes and woodwork.

- A roofed case helps to blend and project the sound and assists in keeping out the dust.

Case design is a rare skill. It is worth taking time to find a suitably experienced designer. A mere fence of bass pipes is not an organ case. Some organ-builders employ their own designers; freelance specialists are also available.

Small organs

The smallest organs are called 'box organs', from their shape. They usually have one manual (row of keys) without pedals, the pipes being placed below the keys and speaking out of the back of the instrument. Although suitable for continuo and choir accompaniment, box organs lack the weight to lead congregational singing except in the very smallest of churches.

Larger one-manual instruments are arranged with the pipes standing over the keys, speaking out above their surroundings. Fitting a pedal keyboard, with or without a low-pitched 16-foot stop, can enhance the bass line of music. An instrument of this type with, say, six stops can lead the singing of a congregation of up to 600 people in a church with a favourably reverberant acoustic (where the sound can be heard dying away for a couple of seconds after the end of a loud chord).

More keyboards

A second manual adds the possibility of instant contrast between the sounds controlled by each keyboard.

Although adding to the complexity and cost of the instrument, a second manual enlarges the available repertoire. It is common for the pipes of the second manual to be enclosed in a 'swellbox', the volume of sound being controlled by a pedal that opens and closes shutters on the front of the box. A second manual does not make the organ significantly louder; it is there for contrast, not power. A third manual adds further flexibility where the

fig. 6
New two-
manual
organ (Peter
Collins)

© Peter Collins

most ambitious music is required. Organs with two or more
manual keyboards also invariably include a pedal keyboard.

Reed stops

Ever since the invention of the organ, larger instruments have
included reed stops, adding to the power of the instrument and
the variety of sound. Reed pipes do, however, need more
frequent tuning than the remainder of the organ.

Mechanism

Most new organs have a mechanical key action, known to
players as 'tracker' action. This is both more reliable and
more responsive than electric or electro-pneumatic key action.
New organs have a moderate key touch, unlike some older
instruments which can be heavy to play. Larger instruments
have electric action to control the stops because 'pistons' can
be provided to help the player change the stops quickly.

chapter 6
Second-hand organs

A second-hand organ may be a good alternative where a church cannot afford a newly made instrument. However, it may not be easy to find one of the right size and shape. A low purchase price may be offset by the need for considerable renovation. If you have an existing instrument, take independent advice to make sure that repair of your existing instrument does not offer better value!

In any event:

● keep to relatively simple instruments with mechanical action; organs with pneumatic action are expensive to move;

● make sure that the organ selected will fit in the space available without significant alteration. Too much alteration can raise the cost to near that of a new instrument.

● Organs more than about 70 years old were not designed to withstand the drying effects of modern winter heating, so their installation is not recommended if a church is heated all week to over 16°C.

The Redundant Organ Rehousing Company Limited (RORCL) maintains a list of redundant organs capable of further use. There tends to be an oversupply of larger organs from former inner-city churches but a lesser supply of smaller instruments. However, the rescue of a historic organ often generates favourable publicity and may attract grants from public bodies.

chapter 7
Electronic instruments

Instruments using electronic simulation of organ sound are extensively advertised and have a much lower initial cost than organs with pipes and the same number of stop controls. Because of their portability and relative lack of bulk, electronic instruments have established a useful place as temporary instruments and as permanent instruments where space is at an absolute premium, such as in village churches absorbed into suburbia. Keyboards are, of course, even more portable but are best used with other instruments as part of a music group.

Electronic instruments are not without problems, however:

- Low initial cost has to be set against a relatively short replacement cycle. Although there are wide variations, published surveys indicate replacement after between ten and twenty-five years, averaging around fifteen years. Do not displace a good existing pipe organ just for short-term savings; at least leave it in position for your successors to restore.

- There are much wider differences in price and quality between one maker and another than there are with organs with pipes.

- The cheaper instruments tend to be much less attractive to musicians than the better ones and may suffer supply difficulties with spare parts.

Loudspeaker boxes

If they are to do their job properly, the loudspeaker boxes required for the reproduction of organ sound need to be much larger than those needed for speech reinforcement or for domestic use. Their accommodation and appearance can be a major problem, especially in a historic building. They can sometimes be hidden in the roof structure, or in the gallery or triforium of a bigger church. Placing the loudspeakers correctly is every bit as important as finding the right position for an organ with pipes. The relatively small extra cost of separating the console from the loudspeakers makes it easy to fall into the trap of combining an east-end console with a west-end source of sound. Such a layout will result in the organ being played too loudly without the organist being aware of the problem.

Bass notes

The proper reproduction of bass notes demands a large diameter loudspeaker and a relatively bulky bass reflex or horn loudspeaker box. However, the ear is unable to detect the direction from which low notes are coming and loudspeakers emitting only deep bass notes can be located in any inconspicuous position.

Loudspeaker appearance

Where concealment in the structure is not practicable it may be necessary to commission purpose-made cabinets to give the loudspeaker boxes an acceptable appearance.

Too often the position and appearance of the loudspeakers are only described in general terms by the maker or installer, and the full implications of their appearance only become apparent after installation. It is essential for the maker to provide proper plans and drawings, showing the proposed position and appearance of the loudspeakers.

It is sometimes suggested that loudspeakers be concealed behind mock organ pipes or even the pipes of a former organ. This is normally unsatisfactory and can be criticized as a deception. It is better to be open about the nature of the instrument being used. In addition, it is all too easy to do considerable damage to the interior of an existing organ when fitting loudspeaker boxes inside it. The existing instrument should either be retained unaltered for future restoration, or else removed to another church, or other suitable building, where it can be cared for and played.

Multiple loudspeakers

It is usual to arrange for the sound of the different manuals to emerge from different sets of loudspeakers. However, if these are moved too far apart, the balance between the manuals will vary markedly with the position of the listener. Some installers try to pick up additional reverberation by arranging multiple loudspeakers, spread all over the church. This is invariably a mistake; both ear and mind expect the sound to come from one place. A good rule is to spread loudspeakers over an area no greater than that occupied by an equivalent organ with pipes.

Consoles

It is worth noting the following points:

● Some instruments are supplied with consoles with stop-tabs instead of the more usual stop-knobs. This system, though cheaper, has real ergonomic disadvantages for the player and has now been abandoned by most traditional organ-builders.

fig. 7
Console with
stop-knobs
© Copeman Hart

24

- The consoles of some electronic instruments are only available with standard cabinetwork designs and finishes, which may not relate well to surrounding furnishings.

- It is also necessary to beware of electronic instruments with untidy vent holes and electrical equipment visible at the back of the console, a relic of the fact that some instruments are primarily produced for home use, where the console is stood against a wall.

- Because all the mechanism is in the console, some electronic instruments occupy nearly as much floor space as a modern small organ with pipes.

Stop lists

Many electronic instruments come with a 'standard' stop list unrelated to the needs of a particular church, so note also the following:

- In order to try to appeal to all tastes, a standard stop list may lack artistic focus and be out of scale with the acoustics of the church.

- An instrument with a cathedral-sized stop list will sound bland and lacking in realism if voiced quietly enough to be bearable in a church of modest dimensions.

- A more natural effect will be achieved from a modest stop-list, with the stops carefully balanced to each other and to the building, than from a vast library of stops chosen at random.

- Sounds generated in computer software are more easily matched to the building than sounds based on 'sampled' (recorded) generation systems.

Demonstrations

Because electronic instruments vary so widely in quality, do not be over-influenced by public demonstrations. Experience has shown that even a poor instrument can sound impressive if well demonstrated. Familiarity over time will reveal its true character. Resist special offers and 'never-to-be-repeated' sales promotions.

Finally, remember that although, in the best electronic instruments, the quality of simulation of organ tone has improved over the years, many musicians still have difficulty in accepting them. This can be a real problem when the time comes to seek a new organist.

chapter 8

Organ-builders

Identify the essential musical and visual issues to be addressed before approaching organ-builders:

- A real comparison of estimates is only possible if organ-builders are asked to respond to the same general brief.

- For substantial work, it is common to obtain quotations from three organ-builders.

- If the comparison is to be meaningful, however, care should be taken to ensure that all are equally qualified for the work proposed.

- Firms of similar standards of work do not differ widely in their charges, so a markedly low price should raise questions as to the scope of the estimate or the competence of the organ-builder.

- It is always desirable to take up references from previous clients.

It is important to employ an organ-builder whose talents match your requirements. The world is becoming an increasingly specialist place and a perfectly competent organ tuner may well not have the expertise or facilities to manufacture a new instrument. An organ-builder who specializes in the restoration of turn-of-the-century instruments may not be ideally suited to work on an organ made before 1850.

Many organ-builders are accredited by the Institute of British Organ Building (IBO). Accreditation covers five categories of work:

- Tuning and Maintenance;

- Cleaning and Overhaul;

- Historic Restoration;

- Rebuilding;

- New Organs.

The criterion is that the organ-builder should be able to undertake the range of work covered by his accreditation with competence and honesty. Accreditation follows inspection of recent work and of workshop premises. The IBO operates a complaints service in relation to the work of accredited organ-builders, and will act as an impartial arbiter in disputes.

Parishes sometimes receive tempting low-cost offers from well-meaning amateurs. Sadly, these should always be refused. Amateurs are unlikely to carry appropriate insurance against damage to the organ and to your building. Unskilled work has led to expensive damage to valuable instruments.

chapter 9
Faculties and advice

Do take outside, independent advice before taking any major decisions. Anglican parishes need legal faculties for any non-routine organ work. The Chancellor in each diocese grants faculties after receiving advice from the Diocesan Advisory Committee for the Care of Churches, generally called the DAC. Each diocese has one or more Diocesan Organ Advisers (DOAs) whose duty is to advise the DAC and the Chancellor and to help parishes to prepare schemes of work that will gain approval. Roman Catholic, Methodist, United Reformed and Baptist churches have their own control systems. To minimize delays it is better to consult at an early stage rather than at the end of your decision process.

Diocesan Organ Advisers are volunteers and do not monitor work, authorize payments or certify completion. Some Anglican dioceses now include organs in the once-every-five-years 'quinquennial' inspection of each church so that parishes have early warning of organ problems.

In more complex cases, the employment of an independent professional consultant/adviser may be helpful. This can be at two levels:

1. an initial appraisal and report on an organ and the recommendation of one scheme of work rather than another;

2. a full supervision of work in progress and certification of payments.

Most professional advisers/consultants are accredited members of the Association of Independent Organ Advisers (AIOA).

chapter 10
Finance, contracts and VAT

Because organ work is required only at infrequent intervals, there may be a desire to plan the work in stages. This is not recommended. It increases costs and leads to a lack of focus in what should be an artistic enterprise. It is far better to make a single effort to do what is reasonable and necessary, and then, tuning apart, forget about the organ for a generation or two.

Stage payments and contracts

Major work is normally invoiced in stages as the work goes along, although the organ-builder will expect a modest down payment with the order. Alarm bells should sound if, however, a down payment of more than 15% is requested. Minor works can be ordered by letter, but major restorations and new organs should be the subject of a proper contract. The IBO publishes a sample contract.

Value added tax

VAT is payable on most organ work. However, an organ in a newly built church, like the building itself, will be zero-rated for VAT. Work on an organ carried out in conjunction with non-trivial alterations to a church that is a listed building will also be zero-rated, providing a faculty has been obtained first. VAT regulations can be changed by government order so it is always wise to enquire about the current position.

chapter 11
Grants

Modest grants may be available from public charities to help fund organ work.

The **Arts Council** has made grants to organs from National Lottery funds, but only where substantial use in public concerts can be expected. The support of the local regional arts council is essential. The **Foundation for Sport and the Arts** has supported organ schemes, especially where a clear public benefit in increased participation in musical events can be demonstrated.

English Heritage has made occasional grants for the repair of organ cases of outstanding historical importance, located in churches that are also themselves historically important. English Heritage does not give grants for the interior workings of organs.

The Heritage Lottery Fund has funds available for the conservation of church furnishings, including organs of particular heritage merit. For grants of up to £50,000, approach the Council for the Care of Churches. For projects requiring grants over £50,000, contact the Heritage Lottery Fund in the first instance before submitting an application.

The **Council for the Care of Churches** administers funds made available by the Pilgrim Trust and others. Modest grants are made towards the restoration of (not alterations to) organs whose historic interest has not been impaired by subsequent alteration.

There are other charities that can include organs in their grant giving. Advice can be obtained from the Council for the Care of Churches and from the British Institute of Organ Studies (BIOS).

Glossary

Action Mechanism that connects the keyboards and the stop controls to the valves that admit the air into the pipes.

Analogue Technology formerly used in electronic instruments to generate simulations of organ sound. Now obsolete and replaced by digital technology.

Bellows Wind storage and control device that has leather moving parts. It may leak, noisily, when very old.

Blower A centrifugal fan that supplies air to the organ under moderate pressure. Usually electrically powered. Needs occasional oiling but very reliable.

Chair case Small organ case placed behind the player, usually on the edge of a gallery.

Cipher Note that sticks 'on', sounding continuously when it should not.

Composition pedal Draws a pre-selected combination of stops when depressed.

Concussion bellows Auxiliary bellows used to steady the wind supply against sudden changes in demand.

Cone tuning System whereby pipes are cut to dead length and then tuned by coning in the top slightly. Gives the most stable tuning.

Console Desk with keyboards and stop controls at which the player sits. May be built in to the front of the organ or detached.

Couplers Enable the pipes of more than one department to be sounded together from one key. Normally the first part of the action to wear.

Digital Computer-related technology now used in almost all electronic instruments.

Electric action Term often used to describe both electro-pneumatic action (see below) and direct electric action, in which the pallet valves that let air into the pipes are operated directly by electro-magnets. Direct electric action is controversial, as not all designs have proved satisfactory.

Electro-pneumatic action Uses low-voltage electricity to link keys with organ and for the coupling action, combined with pneumatic mechanism to actually open the pallet valves that let air into the pipes.

Feeder bellows An auxiliary bellows, generally found under the main bellows of older organs, which is an essential part of hand blowing. Not required if an electric blower is fitted.

Flue pipes (e.g. stops labelled Open Diapason, Principal, Stopped Diapason) The most common type of pipe in the organ, working rather like a recorder or whistle. Can vary in length between ¾ inch and 32 feet.

Front pipes Bass pipes on show in the organ case. Some smaller pipes, put in to complete the pattern, may be dummy. Front pipes may be made in lead alloy (often gilded), zinc (often painted) or, in modern organs, polished tin alloy.

Humidifier Device to feed moist air into the interior of an organ to protect wooden mechanism from splits and warping caused by low humidity from continuous winter heating. Requires maintenance. Not required in modern instruments.

Key-touch The feel of the keys, important to players. Too heavy a touch is tiring but some electric and pneumatic action touches are too light. Mechanical 'tracker' action has a touch with a natural initial resistance which gives players confidence.

Manual Keys played with the hands, as opposed to keys played with the feet.

Melodic bass Caters for players who cannot manage the pedals by playing a sub-foundation stop on the lowest note of any chord held on the manual. Available on some organs with electric or pneumatic action and on some electronic instruments.

MIDI A standard for the inter-communication of electrically controlled musical instruments. Has not proved very useful with organs as it has difficulty in coping with the complexities of the instrument.

Motor Tiny leather-covered bellows that uses air pressure to open a valve in the mechanism. When leather eventually fails, notes play slowly or not at all.

Mouth Opening in the front of a pipe where the sound vibration is initially generated. Vulnerable to physical damage.

Murmur A pipe sounding softly all the time because of a partial leak of air from the soundboard.

Pallet Leather-faced valve that controls the admission of air to the pipe.

Pedal-board Pedal keys and their frame. Plays the bass notes of the organ. The design of pedal-boards varies considerably and can be controversial.

Pipe-shade Ornament, often carved or fretted, which fills the space between the tops of the front pipes and the upper cornice of the organ case.

Pistons Small buttons which, when pressed, draw pre-selected combinations of stops. Placed between the keyboards or above the pedal-board. Require electric or pneumatic mechanism to operate.

Pneumatic action Short for tubular pneumatic action. The keys are linked to the interior by lead tubes conveying small amounts of wind that trigger the mechanism in the soundboards.

Purse Leather diaphragm that has a similar function to that of a 'motor'.

Reed pipes (e.g. stops labelled Trumpet, Oboe, Clarinet) Have vibrating brass tongues which initiate the sound. Louder and more colourful than flue pipes but more trouble to make and voice.

Reservoir A large bellows. Formerly used to store wind between the strokes of hand blowing, now used to control the flow from an electric blower and to cushion sudden changes in demand. Bellows with two sets of ribs to give extra capacity are known as 'double-rise'. Cast-iron weights on the top of the reservoir control the pressure and often show the initials of the builder.

Roller A bar of wood or metal which, in twisting, transmits the motion of the key action sideways, enabling the pipes to be placed in a different order to the keys. The rollers are mounted together on a **rollerboard**. Often visible if the music desk is removed.

Running A pipe that sounds unbidden because wind has leaked from the mechanism feeding an adjacent pipe.

Sampling Technique used in some electronic instruments whereby short recordings of selected organ pipes form the basis of the simulation.

Sequencer Generally a facility whereby a very large number of pre-selected combinations of stops can be stored in the organ mechanism and brought into operation successively by pressing a 'next' piston. Confusingly, this name is also sometimes applied to a mechanism that stores the notes of a complete piece of music, enabling the organ to perform without a player being present. This is sometimes fitted to electronic instruments and to organs with electric or electro-pneumatic key action.

Slide Perforated slide in the soundboard that controls whether a given rank of pipes is in use. Connected to a stop-knob on the console.

Software-generation System used in better-grade electronic instruments. Voicing is readily adjustable in the building.

Soundboard Something of a misnomer. A large flat box on which the pipes stand and which contains the mechanism that supplies them with air.

Stop-knobs Controls on the organ console, normally placed on jambs either side of the keys, which are drawn out to bring on ranks of pipes.

Stop-tabs Also known as stop-keys. These control ranks of pipes in the same way as stop-knobs. Usually placed under the music desk. Obsolescent but still used in cheaper electronic instruments.

Swellbox Heavily constructed timber box covering all the pipes of a department of the organ. The volume of sound is controlled by opening the louvres connected to a 'swell pedal' on the console.

Swell pedal Lever on the console which controls the opening of the swellbox. Can either be pivoted ('balanced pedal') and placed in the centre of the board above the pedal keys, or a lever on the right-hand side which is depressed to open the swellbox.

Tower The part of an organ case where the largest pipes are grouped together, often arranged in a projecting V or semi-circle.

Tracker Thin strip of wood that transmits the motion of the key to the interior of an organ with mechanical action. The name has come to be applied to the whole action (tracker action) and even to the whole organ (tracker organ). By far the most common action in both old and new organs.

Transformer-rectifier Device that takes in mains-voltage current and delivers safe low-voltage current for electrically operated action mechanism.

Tremulant Device that provides a regular variation in the wind supply, causing a distinctive modulation in the sound of a solo stop. Not unlike a singer's vibrato.

Tuning slide Sleeve of thin tinned steel (occasionally of aluminium), which is sprung on to the top of the pipe. The organ tuner can move the slide up and down to vary the pitch but the tuning is less stable than if cone tuning is used.

Wind pressure Varies between about 50 mm (2 in) water gauge in the smallest organs to 250 mm (10 in) or more in the largest cathedral organs. An important design parameter.

appendix 2
References

Peter Hurford, *Making Music on the Organ*, Oxford University Press, 1990.

Nicholas Thistlethwaite and Geoffrey Webber, *New Cambridge Companion to the Organ*, Cambridge University Press, 1998.

David Baker, *The Organ*, Princes Risborough, Shire Publications, 1991.

Peter Williams and Barbara Owen, 'The organ', *The New Grove Dictionary of Musical Instruments*, Macmillan, London, 1988.

John Norman, *The Organs of Britain*, Newton Abbot, David & Charles, 1984.

Cecil Clutton and Austin Niland, *The British Organ*, London, Eyre Methuen, 1982.

John Newman, *A Review of the Ecclesiastical Exemption from Listed Building Controls*, Department for Culture, Media & Sport and the Welsh Office, 1997.

OrganBuilding, IBO. Available from 13 Ryefields, Thurston, Suffolk IP31 3TD (Annual journal).

Many of these books are no longer in print but may be available second-hand or in public libraries.

Useful addresses and websites

Association of Independent Organ Advisers (AIOA)
39 Church Street, Haslingfield, Cambridge CB3 7JE
www.aioa.org.uk

British Institute of Organ Studies (BIOS)
39 Church Street, Haslingfield, Cambridge CB3 7JE
www.bios.org.uk

Council for the Care of Churches (CCC)
Church House, Great Smith Street, London SW1P 3NZ
www.churchcare.co.uk/ccc

English Heritage
23 Savile Row, London W1X 1AB
www.english-heritage.org.uk

Foundation for Sport and the Arts
PO Box 20, Liverpool L13 1HB

Institute of British Organ Building (IBO)
13 Ryefields, Thurston, Suffolk IP31 3TD
www.ibo.co.uk

National Pipe Organ Register (NPOR)
www.bios.org.uk/npor.html

Redundant Organ Rehousing Company Limited (RORCL)
Acorns Rising, Gladestry, Kington HR5 3NT
www.rorcl.co.uk

Royal College of Organists (RCO)
7 St Andrew's Street, London EC4A 3LQ
www.rco.org.uk

Royal School of Church Music (RSCM)
Cleveland Lodge, Dorking RH5 6BW
www.rscm.com

Index